An Album of
THE GREAT WAVE
of
IMMIGRATION

By April Koral

FRANKLIN WATTS
NEW YORK   CHICAGO   LONDON   TORONTO   SYDNEY

*To Kira and
Thea with love*

Cover photograph copyright ©: National Park Service, Ellis Island Immigration Museum

Photographs copyright ©: National Park Service, Ellis Island Immigration Museum: pp. 4, 6 bottom, 18 bottom, 22 bottom, 23, 26 top, 26 bottom, 29 bottom, 34 top, 35 center, 35 bottom, 43 top, 43 center, 48 inset, 52 top left, 57 top (both), 57 bottom right; The Bettmann Archive: pp. 6 top, 29 top, 35 top, 38 center, 43 bottom, 44 top, 44 bottom, 45 top, 52 top right; New York Public Library, Picture Collection: pp. 6 center, 11 left, 16, 22 top, 22 center, 34 bottom, 38 bottom, 39 top, 41, 44 center, 45 bottom, 55 top; UPI/Bettmann Newsphotos: pp. 8 top (both), 52 center, 55 bottom; Library of Congress: pp. 8 bottom left, 9, 15, 18 top; National Park Service, Augustus Sherman Collection: pp. 8 bottom right, 10 top, 10 center right, 10 bottom, 11 right, 28 top, 29 center, 48, 57 bottom left; New York Public Library, Local History Division: pp. 10 center left, 38 top; New York Public Library, Special Collections/Lewis Hine: pp. 25 top, 34 center, 39 bottom; The National Archives: pp. 25 bottom, 26 center, 28 center, 31; The George Eastman House/Lewis Hine: p. 28 bottom; North Wind Picture Archives, Alfred, ME: p. 52 bottom; The Balch Institute for Ethnic Studies Library: pp. 56 top (Matz Family Photographs), 56 center (Ricci Family Photographs), 56 bottom (La Colonia Italiana Photographs); U.S. Department of Justice, Immigration & Naturalization Service: p. 58.

Library of Congress Cataloging-in-Publication Data

Koral, April.
An album of the great wave of immigration / by April Koral.
p.   cm.—(Picture album)
Includes bibliographical references (p.   ) and index.
Summary: A pictorial history of the large wave of immigration that occurred in the United States from 1890 to 1924.
ISBN 0-531-11123-7
1. United States—Emigration and immigration—History—Juvenile literature.   2. United States—Emigration and immigration—History—Pictorial works.   [1. United States—Emigration and immigration—History.]   I. Title.   II. Series.
JV6453.K67   1992
304.8′73—dc20   92-15009 CIP AC

Contents

Chapter One

LEAVING HOME

They left home and family. Sometimes they traveled with a parent, a sister or a brother, or a friend. Often they came alone. Many had never been beyond the small town or city in which they were born, and knew little of the United States and its way of life. Most did not speak English. Most did not know what kind of job they would get or where they would live.

These were the immigrants who landed on America's shores between 1890 and 1924. They were part of what was to become the largest wave of immigration in the history of the nation. Many returned home—but many more stayed.

Most of these newcomers came from southern and eastern Europe—Italy, Poland, Russia, Austria, Hungary, Greece, and Turkey. (The immigrants who had come to the United States before were mostly from northern Europe— the British Isles, Germany, Scandinavia, and Holland.)

Why did they come? Some came simply for adventure or to avoid military service. Others, such as Jewish immigrants from Poland and Russia and Armenians from Turkey,

These Polish Jews stand amid the rubble of what was once their home.

Representatives of a Russian village struck by famine come to get seed for planting crops the following season. Economic hardships such as this forced many to emigrate.

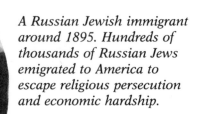

A Russian Jewish immigrant around 1895. Hundreds of thousands of Russian Jews emigrated to America to escape religious persecution and economic hardship.

were escaping persecution and even death. But most of the immigrants were fleeing poverty. They had heard that America was the land of opportunity. Indeed, opportunity was to be found—manning the assembly lines of bustling factories, digging in coal mines, and laying railroad track. Many people dreamed of owning their own businesses. Harry Glassman left the poverty of Mogilev, Russia, and opened a dry-goods store with his wife, Rebecca, in Carney, Oklahoma. Max Winagrad fled Antopol, Poland, and worked in a shoe factory in New York City before going into business selling dresses imported from Europe.

The more who came, the more people back in the old country imagined that the promises of a better life were within their reach, too. Immigrants frequently sent money and food to relatives still in Europe, and many times helped them emigrate by paying the boat passage. Occasionally, immigrants returned for a visit looking prosperous and with money in their pockets.

The largest number of immigrants who came to the United States during this great wave of immigration were from Italy. In the late 1800s, an Italian described the situation in his country in a letter to a friend who lived in the United States:

Things go badly here. Many contadini [peasants] here do not eat bread. They live on potatoes and beans. . . . One can only find work three or four months of the year. Why do so many go to America? Because they are better off there. . . . When someone returns from America to tell us that the wages are superior and that there are fewer discomforts, many of the men cannot resist the temptation to go and find out for themselves.[1]

Polish refugees from the towns surrounding Warsaw wait in the quarantine station at Danzig, Poland, for boats sailing to America.

An Italian mother and her tired children wait patiently for their chance to leave for America.

An Italian piper emigrates.

Most of the Italian immigrants were from the southern part of the country, which was desperately poor. Over the years, forests had been cut down and the rain had carried away topsoil and created swamps. Much of the land was owned by landlords who lived elsewhere and didn't want to spend money to improve the soil. The farmers could barely produce enough on their small plots of land to feed themselves and their families. To make matters worse, a cholera epidemic had killed over 55,000 people and the swamps were breeding malaria, another serious disease.

By the late 1800s, Florida and California had begun to grow fruits such as lemons and oranges, competing with the Italian farmers who shipped produce here. Italian winemakers were also suffering because France put a high tariff (a kind of tax) on all Italian wines coming into France, which made their product more expensive.

Many of the Italian immigrants were young men who hoped to return home after they had saved enough money. Others went back and forth, going back when they could not find work in America. Some workers came through the *padrone* system. The *padrone* were men who found unskilled laborers in Italy for businesses in the United States. Although the *padrone* guaranteed the immigrants work, the pay was often pitifully low.

More Italians arrived into the new world than any other nationality.

Many immigrant families followed husbands and fathers to America.

A young Russian Jewish girl, one of the many Russian immigrants to arrive between 1890 and 1924

A sixteen-year-old soldier who had seen action in World War I was "adopted" by the U.S. Army and made an honorary sergeant.

These eight children were orphaned when their mother was killed in a Russian massacre.

This mother and child are marked as immigrants by their peasant garb and their expressions of hope, fear, and patience.

This English mother is willing to make the difficult trip with her six children.

Whereas the Italian immigrant was motivated by economic forces, the Jewish immigrant was pushed by other reasons as well. Between 1881 and 1914, nearly 2 million Jews came to the United States, most from Russia and Poland. Sometimes husbands came first and families followed, but more often entire families came. Although Jews had been living in these countries for centuries, they had often been the victims of religious persecution.

By the late 1800s, hundreds of thousands of Russian Jews had been driven from their homes and been forced to live in an area in the western part of Russia called the Pale of Settlement. Many were terribly poor. They worked in small shops and factories or made livings as traders, storekeepers, and peddlers.

By the late 1800s, more and more laws were passed to make life miserable for these people. They were not allowed to worship freely, own land, or go into certain professions. Only a small number were allowed to continue their education past elementary school. Jewish boys were forced into the czar's army as teenagers and had to stay for as long as twenty-five years!

Organized attacks on Jews, called *pogroms*, had also become more and more common in Poland and Russia. Mobs beat and killed Jews, and Jewish homes and property were destroyed. The leaders of the attacks went unpunished. In fact, local police stood by and watched. Tens of thousands of Jews were victims of this cruel violence.

It's no wonder that unlike immigrants from Italy, the Jewish immigrants never considered returning to their former homes. Dr. George Price, a Jewish immigrant, described his feelings toward his homeland in a diary written in 1882.

> *Sympathy for Russia? How ironic it sounds! Am I not despised? . . . Can I even think that someone considers me a human being capable of thinking and feeling like others? Do I not rise daily with the fear lest the hungry mob attack me? . . . It is impossible . . . that a Jew should regret leaving Russia.*[2]

Armenian immigrants were fleeing persecution and terror of an even greater magnitude. Many of the Armenians who lived in Turkey in the late 1800s dreamed of forming their own nation. The Turkish sultan reacted to these wishes for independence by ordering the massacre of the Armenians. Millions of men, women, and children died. Those who escaped went to Russia, Iran, and the United States. Many of those who arrived here settled in California; others made their homes in New Jersey and New York.

The third largest group of immigrants were the Slavs. This group included Poles, Bohemians, Ukrainians, Slovaks, Russians, Bulgarians, Serbs, Croatians, Montenegrins, and Slovenians. In all, as many as 4 million Slavs left home, mostly because of unemployment or because they could not support themselves and their families on their small plots of land. Many of these immigrants worked for several years in America and then returned home and bought more land with money they had saved.

The Greeks came, too. As was the situation in southern Italy, Greece had never had good soil. And erosion caused by hundreds of years of cutting down trees had further swept away the topsoil, making it more difficult for Greek farmers to survive.

Greek families saved their money, sold land or farm animals, or even borrowed so that a father or son could go to the United States. Most of the Greek arrivals were men who planned to return home. Some came in order to save enough for a dowry for the family's daughters. (A dowry is the money or property brought by a bride to her bridegroom at marriage.) In Greece during that time, it was hard for a woman to get married without a dowry.

Immigrants from Sweden and Norway, many of them unable to make a living on their small farms, went to Minnesota, South Dakota, and other midwestern states to become farmers.

Finally, the British also continued to come to the United States in large numbers. Between 1870 and 1900, nearly 3 million arrived here.

Most of the immigrants from the British Isles were different from the majority of other immigrants who were crowding America's shores. They did not come looking for just any work. Instead, they had specific skills that they knew were in demand here and that paid well. Many expected to return home with savings—and did. Through the 1800s, for example, they went to the mill towns in New England, working as expert spinners, weavers, dyers, printers, draftsmen, and designers.

When economic conditions became particularly bad in England, unskilled laborers also came. In the 1870s, American farmers began selling their grain in England. This brought down the price that English farmers could get for their wheat. Workers lost jobs and many looked for work in the United States. During bad times, some industries even encouraged their workers to emigrate. In 1879, the North Wales Miners' Association offered 7 pounds (about $32) to any member who would go to America to work as a coal miner.

People also approached America from other shores. About 350,000 blacks came from the Caribbean islands between 1880 and 1924. Hundreds of thousands of Mexicans came to California, Arizona, New Mexico, and Texas. Some Mexicans came legally; others just walked across the border.

Japanese workers, students, and merchants also emigrated to the United States, landing in California and Hawaii (Hawaii was then a United States territory). In Hawaii, the Japanese did the backbreaking work of harvesting sugarcane. Japan was suffering from unemployment and its government was not against exporting some of its workers.

Not all nations wanted their citizens to leave. In 1903, Hungary passed a law that prohibited public speeches and advertisements recommending emigration. Its government even gave money to immigrants who wanted to return home.

The Greek government threatened not to allow anyone under the age of sixteen or anyone who had not done his military service to leave. Greek newspapers also wrote articles on how difficult life was in America, often printing letters of complaints from Greek immigrants.

Despite the promise of a better life, many mothers and fathers also didn't want their children to leave home. A son could help his father in the fields or in business. More im-

A small number of black immigrants, most from the Caribbean, emigrated to the United States during this period.

portant, parents knew they might never see their children again. Few immigrants could afford a vacation back home, and there were no telephones. Separating from one's family was very painful.

Marcus Ravage, who emigrated from Russia, remembers the weeks before leaving:

> *In the evening when we were alone together my mother would . . . gaze into my eyes as if she tried to absorb enough of me to last her for the coming months of absence. "You will write us, dear?" she kept asking continually. . . .*
>
> *At the moment of departure, when the train drew into the station, she lost control of her feelings. As she embraced me for the last time her sobs became violent and father had to separate us. There was a despair in her way of clinging to me which I could not then understand. I understand it now. I never saw her again.*[3]

This collage of immigrant faces illustrates the diversity of the immigrant population. Clockwise from the top left: a Rumanian, a Norwegian, an Austrian, a Hungarian, another Hungarian, and a Russian.

The sad good-byes were the same for everyone, no matter what country they came from. An Italian immigrant who came when he was twenty-two could never forget the pain of leaving his family.

> *My heart aches every time I think about that afternoon when I left my parents and friends to go to the railroad station. My mother kissed me good-bye and then stood by the doorway stiff as a statue sobbing as my father and I left the house. At the station even my father as hard as he tried could not keep the tears from filling his eyes.*[4]

In the weeks after the immigrants departed, there would be little time for them to think about friends and family. By the time they reached the ships that would take them to America, they were often already exhausted. Many would cross borders illegally in the middle of the night, walk miles with a bundle of clothes on their back, or sit for hours and hours in a slow-moving, airless railroad car crammed with other immigrants. But the trip of their life was the one they were about to take—across the 3,000-mile ocean that separated them from their new lives.

Immigrants traveling in steerage around 1900, the peak period of immigration

Chapter Two
THE
TRIP
AND
ARRIVAL

An "unforgettable" experience. That's how many turn-of-the-century immigrants have described their trip across the Atlantic. The voyage that these men, women, and children took to their new homes lasted anywhere from eight days to two weeks, depending on the weather. (Before steamships came into use in the late 1800s, boats used sails and a trip across the Atlantic would take anywhere from one to three months!) For some of these travelers, the voyage could be quite pleasant. First-class passengers, for example, dined on good food in spacious and elegant dining rooms, enjoyed the service of attentive waiters, and danced to the rhythms of famous orchestras. At night, they slept in comfortable cabins with windows.

Far below, in an area at the bottom of the boat called *steerage*, the poorer immigrants were having a very different experience. One thousand or more men, women, and children were packed into rows of narrow bunk beds. There were no portholes to let in air or light, and the ceiling was only 6 to 8 feet high (1.8–2.4 m). Hundreds of people had to share only a handful of toilets, and there were even fewer showers.

Most of these immigrants had never been on such a large ship and were terrified by the pounding of the waves against the sides of the ship, the roar of the engines, and the tossing back and forth. Many immediately became seasick and stayed that way for the rest of the trip. People vomited on the floor; with each passing day, the smell became worse and worse. When there was a storm, women and children cried. Others prayed.

"I don't even like to think about that trip," says Bessie Fingerman, who was nine years old when she came to the United States from Russia in 1912. "It took my father seven years to save enough money to send for my mother and sister and brother. The trip took a week and it was a horror. We were the sickest people on the boat. Some first-class passengers heard about us and sent down some fruit. My mother told me I was so sick that I threw up worms."

In many of the ships, there was no dining room for steerage passengers; there weren't even tables to eat on. Some people brought along their own food. Those who didn't had to go up to the deck, where food was dished out into a bucket, which they then brought downstairs. The food that the immigrants were served was horrible. One of the common foods was herring, which was cheap and could last throughout the trip without spoiling. It was not unusual for steerage passengers to eat little more than bread for the entire trip.

A large percentage of the ships with immigrants aboard landed in New York City. When the ship slowed and the roar of the engines died down, everyone crowded onto the deck. Around them, the harbor was filled with other boats waiting to dock. At the first sight of America, children were lifted onto their parents' shoulders. People shouted with excitement and cried from relief and happiness.

First- and second-class passengers not only enjoyed better life on the boat, but were treated better by American immigration officials, who decided who would be allowed into the country. Once the boat was in New York Harbor, immigration officials boarded, gave a quick medical exam to these passengers, and asked a few polite questions. Then they were welcomed to America.

It was another story for steerage passengers.

Before 1892, the immigrants were taken to Castle Garden, an old stone castle in lower Manhattan. But Castle Garden couldn't possibly handle the growing number of immigrants, and in 1892 the U.S. government built a center to process immigrants on Ellis Island in New York Harbor. All of the new center's buildings were made of wood, and in 1897 they all burned to the ground. Three years later, the new Ellis Island was built. It was a vast place, with dining halls, a hospital, a post office, and a railroad ticket office. Although Ellis Island was only one of seventy receiving stations in the country at the time, 90 percent of all immigrants passed through its doors, sometimes thousands in one day. For many, it was an unforgettable introduction to their new home.

Ellis Island immigration officials tried to process the newcomers as quickly as possible—the average stay was only three to five hours—but it was a hectic place. A sign that read "Immigrants must be treated with kindness and consideration" was hung on the walls—but workers often did not pay attention to it. People were sometimes pushed from one room to another or were yelled at to keep them moving. The immigrants were often exhausted from the long trip, and although excited, they were also nervous. Would they be allowed into America? Some had no homes to go back to; most had sold everything they owned.

In order to be allowed into the United States, the immigrants had to pass a number of tests. To begin with, they had

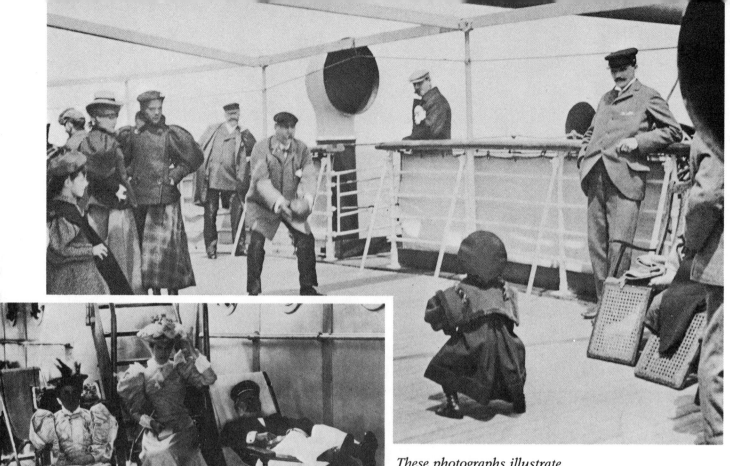

These photographs illustrate
the difference in the way
immigrants traveling in
steerage, and these immigrants,
traveling in first class,
fared on the voyage.

Castle Garden, 1880–1890, the old Ellis Island

Arriving at Ellis Island, a family hurries to the next stage in the long process for entry to their new home.

Marriageable young women arriving for processing on Ellis Island

Immigrants stare longingly at the distant Statue of Liberty, shrouded in fog.

to be in good health. Unknown to them, their examination started as soon as they arrived. Right after entering what was called the Main Building, the immigrants walked up a long flight of steps carrying their hand luggage. From the top of the stairs, a group of medical inspectors watched them carefully. The doctors studied each immigrant—skin, face, the way of walking—to see if they could spot an illness or handicap. Those people who were suspected of having a health problem were taken aside and their clothing was marked with chalk—L for lameness, Ft for foot problems, H for possible heart trouble, C for conjunctivitis (an eye problem). They were then sent to other doctors to be examined more closely.

After this, everyone entered a huge room known as the Great Hall, in which thousands of immigrants were crowded. First, all of the immigrants were examined for trachoma, a contagious eye disease that was common among the European immigrants. There was no cure for trachoma in those days, and anyone who had it was immediately sent back home.

Even before they arrived at Ellis Island, many immigrants had heard about this exam. A doctor used a small hook to raise the immigrant's upper eyelid. Elda Willitts, who came from the town of Lucca, in Italy, as a child in 1916, found out about the dreaded exam on the boat to New York City. She recalled:

> *A man who had traveled back and forth between Europe and the United States took me on a walk one day and he said, "You know what? When you get over to Ellis Island they're going to be examining your eyes with a hook. Don't let them do it because you know what? They did it to me—and one eye fell in my pocket."*[1]

These Slavic immigrants did not know, as they carried their bundles up the stairs for processing, that their medical examinations had already begun. Doctors were observing them for ailments from the top of the stairs.

A U.S. Public Health Service official examines an immigrant's eyes.

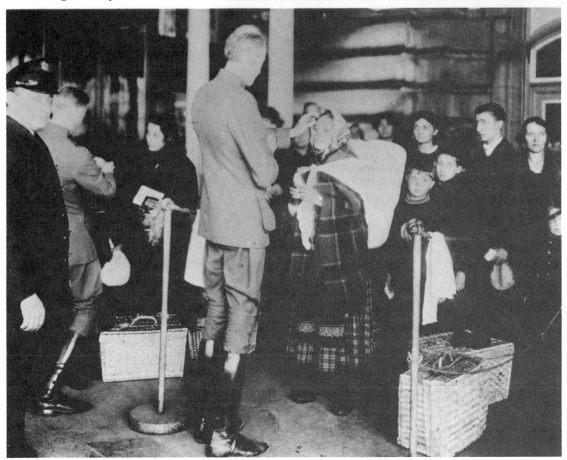

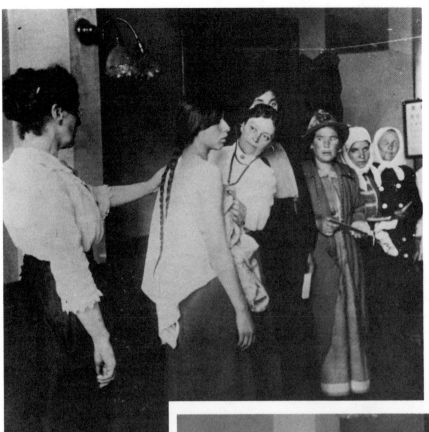

A young woman getting a chest exam as part of her medical inspection on Ellis Island

Another part of the medical examination was a mental test.

An immigrant identification card issued on Ellis Island

After the medical exam, the immigrants were interviewed by an immigration inspector, who asked a long series of questions. After getting such basic information as name, age, and occupation, the inspectors asked the immigrants other questions: "Do you believe in polygamy?" (marrying more than one person), "Do you advocate the overthrow of the government by force?," and "Have you ever been in prison?"

The immigrants were also asked if they already had a job in the United States. In both 1885 and 1887, laws were passed by Congress that forbade contract laborers from coming into the United States. A contract laborer was anyone who had had a job arranged for him before arriving. What should the immigrant answer? On the one hand, he wanted to show that he would not become a public charge (not be able to support himself), which was grounds for deportation. On the other hand, he did not want to seem to have too definite a job because then it would appear that it had been arranged in his home country!

Approximately 2 percent of all would-be immigrants were not allowed into the United States. That doesn't sound like much, but it could mean as many as 1,000 people a month. A person with a slight limp or a deformed hand would often be rejected immediately, even though he or she was strong and healthy and had been a hard worker back home. A person who spoke very slowly might be mistakenly declared mentally retarded and rejected. For each of those people and their families, it was a heartbreaking experience. Anyone could be rejected—a mother, father, child, or grandparent. Most of the time, the family had little choice but to let the one family member return by himself or, in the case of a child, with a parent or sibling, to their old home. Many times, they never saw him or her again. It is no wonder that Ellis Island came to be known as the "Island of Tears."

These Slavic women are wearing labels that were probably either identification cards issued on board ship or railway passes bought after processing on Ellis Island.

These immigrant men wait for their processing.

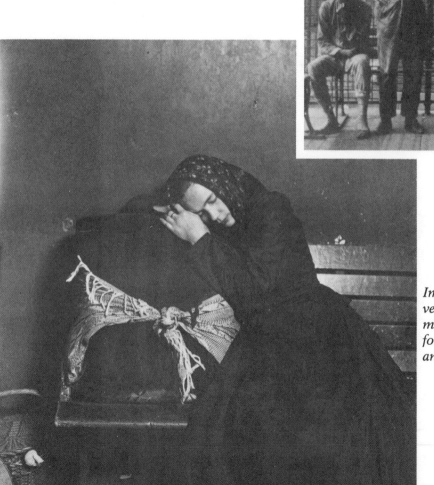

Immigrants like this very tired woman spent many hours waiting for inspections and questionings.

One of the classrooms
on Ellis Island where
immigrants were given
instructions before their
admittance to the
United States

A children's playground
on the roof garden
of Ellis Island

Newly arrived
immigrants
in the communal
dining room on
Ellis Island

Women traveling alone had an especially hard time getting through Ellis Island. In those days, women were not expected to make trips by themselves and there was suspicion against any woman who was not under the "protection" of a father, brother, or other male family member. Sometimes, they were even accused of being prostitutes. Unlike men traveling alone to the United States, women had to either be met by a relative, a husband-to-be (and married immediately!), a representative of a social service organization, or a sponsor who agreed to support her until she found a job—and that sponsor could not be a man!

Some women came as so-called "picture brides." Men who lived in the United States and wanted to marry a woman from back home would correspond with a woman, who would then send a picture of herself. If their letter romance seemed to be going well, the woman would cross the Atlantic prepared to marry the man. These romances, of course, sometimes ended abruptly. The husband-to-be might have had a change of heart and might not show up to meet the boat. Other times the woman, after meeting her husband-to-be in person, decided she'd rather take the next boat back home.

The immigrants who were not staying in New York City bought railroad tickets at the ticket office on Ellis Island. They were often put on old and dilapidated special immigration trains. To make matters worse, although the immigrants paid first-class fares, they were often sold roundabout routes so that it took twice as long as necessary to get where they were going. The railroad agents were supposed to divide the immigrants' business among the twelve railroads that operated out of New York City, but an immigrant who was going to Chicago, for example, might be sent south through Norfolk, Virginia. There were also unintentional mix-ups. One group of Italians wanted to go to Amsterdam Avenue in New York City and ended up on a train to Amsterdam, a city in upstate New York!

Once the processing was completed, and the immigrants had been admitted to the United States, many rode a ferry such as this one to the railroad terminals in Hoboken and Jersey City, New Jersey.

When the immigrants stepped onto American soil, what most faced was different from everything they had ever known. Many would end up working in factories, doing repetitious work from early morning until late at night. Many had lived in the country; now they would be crowded into tiny, airless apartments. They had left all that was familiar to them—towns in which they not only knew each house but who lived in it. Here, everyone was a stranger. It would test all their abilities—their intelligence, their physical strength, their patience, and their courage—to make this unknown land someplace they could call home.

Chapter Three
THE
IMMIGRANTS
AT
WORK
AND AT
HOME

From the moment the immigrants stepped off the boat, they had one goal—finding a job.

By the late 1800s, the farming land in America's western and southern states had been settled, some by previous immigrants, and the country was now turning its energies to building its cities and manufacturing goods. There were plenty of factory jobs, especially in the East and Northeast. And there was always a job for a man who was willing to do the backbreaking work of a laborer—digging coal, laying railroad tracks, or paving streets.

A job in those days did not mean working from nine o'clock in the morning until five o'clock at night with an hour off for lunch and a two-week paid vacation. Most workers at that time were treated terribly—but the immigrants, who could not speak English well and were desperate to work— were exploited the most. Men and women alike were often forced to work ten and eleven hours a day. In addition, there were no laws to protect people from unhealthy or dangerous working conditions. In return for a tiny weekly paycheck on which the immigrants could hardly make ends meet, they might be robbed of their health or even their life.

Sometimes, children were forced to work to help pay the bills and so that their family would have enough to eat. Although there were some laws against child labor, they were often ignored. Pauline Newman, who came from Lithuania in 1901, was only eight years old when she took a job in a factory that made shirts. Her pay was $1.50 a week. She recalled:

> *We started at seven-thirty in the morning and during the busy season we worked until nine in the evening. They didn't pay you any overtime. . . . The employers were always tipped off if there was going to be an inspection. "Quick," they'd say, "into the boxes!" And we children would climb into the big boxes the finished shirts were stored in. Then some shirts were piled on top of us, and when the inspector came—no children.*[1]

For everyone, conditions in the factories were terrible. Bosses watched over the workers, and many employers did not allow workers to talk to the people sitting next to them. In some factories, workers were even limited as to how often they could go to the bathroom and how much time they could spend there. The factory owners were determined to squeeze as much work as they possibly could out of these poor men, women, and children. It was not uncommon for employers to post a sign that said, "If you don't come in on Sunday, don't come in on Monday." In other words, if the boss had work that needed to be done, you were expected to work seven days a week.

Finding a job was one of the first priorities of the new immigrants. Many went to work on the railroads, as did the men pictured here.

Others (above) worked harvesting crops, like the beet harvesters here.

Immigrants with skills held jobs like this French worker, who is making tapestries.

*A Chinese butcher and grocery shop around
1900 in San Francisco's Chinatown*

*Special emigrant
cars were set
aside on the
railroads. This
ticket carried
the passenger
from Chicago to
San Francisco.*

*Travel agencies advertised jobs for immigrants. Many had
to travel across the country in order to find work.*

A reader of the *Forward*, a Jewish newspaper, complained to the editor in 1906:

> *Dear Editor,*
>
> *. . . We work in a Bleeker Street shop, where we make raincoats. With us is a thirteen-year-old boy who works hard for the $2.50 dollars [a week] he earns.*
>
> *Just lately it happened that the boy came to work ten minutes late. This was a "crime" the bosses couldn't overlook, and for the lost ten minutes they docked him two cents.*[2]

Being docked (having some wages taken away) or being fired might mean not having enough money to pay the rent or even to buy milk for the family's children. And when people lost their jobs, there was no unemployment insurance, no welfare, and no pensions.

The children especially suffered from the poverty. Babies died because parents could not afford to take them to the doctor. Each year, thousands of sick and homeless children were found by the police on the streets of New York City.

Many young children worked during the day and went to school at night. Jacob Riis, a photographer, described one such little girl named Susie who lived in Manhattan at the turn of the century and spent her days at home pasting together tin boxes:

> *Little Susie . . . is a type of the tenement-house children whose work begins early and ends late. Her shop is her home. Every morning she drags down [from her apartment] . . . heavy bundles of the little tin boxes much too heavy*

for her twelve years, and when she has fin-
ished running errands and earning a few pen-
nies that way, takes her place at the bench
and pastes two hundred before it is time for
evening school. Then she has earned sixty
cents—"More than Mother," she says with a
smile. . . .[3]

Immigrants took any work they could find. Many Italians worked as laborers, building railroads, tunnels, subways, and streets. One story tells of an Italian immigrant who said: "Well, I came to America because I heard the streets were paved with gold. When I got here, I found out three things: first, the streets weren't paved with gold; second, they weren't paved at all; and third, I was expected to pave them."

Italians also opened candy stores and fruit stands, worked as barbers, and made and sold artificial flowers. Older men tried to make money as organ grinders, walking the streets all day and into the night. Young boys shined shoes.

Although the Greeks, too, were farmers at home, they were attracted to large cities where they could find friends from the old country and jobs. Many started out as street peddlers, selling fruits and vegetables or shining shoes. Others worked in factories and railroad construction gangs.

The Jewish immigrants were often skilled workers. About half were in the clothing business, working at sewing machines at home and in factories. They also started out as peddlers, selling everything from eggs to buttons and thread. In addition, numerous Jewish writers, poets, playwrights, actors, actresses, and singers created a rich cultural life in their communities.

Thousands of immigrants worked in the coal mines. Working and living conditions for the miners were harsh.

Children worked with their families at home to provide needed income. Here they're making artificial flowers; they were paid 6 cents for 144 flowers.

Two mothers and their children doing "piece work" in their New York tenement apartments. One family made gloves while the other made clothing.

These children were paid 60 cents a day for making tin boxes.

Many other boys roamed the streets selling newspapers.

The mines were usually in isolated areas, and the miners had no choice but to buy their food from overpriced stores owned by the mining company. The miners sometimes lived in wooden shacks with no running water, little heat in the winter, and beds with straw mattresses. But because they were afraid of being fired, few complained.

George Palochek came from Czechoslovakia in 1912 when he was seventeen years old and started working in the mines. He was paid $2.15 a week for ten hours of work a day, six days a week, and he had to buy his own tools. The company charged him seven cents a day for the use of a lamp. He and his fellow workers also had to walk for an hour in order to get to work.

Most mine owners not only cared little about their workers' comfort, but they also had little consideration for their safety. Indeed, George Palochek recalled that the lives of mules, who carried the coal out of the mines, were more valuable to the mine owners than those of their human workers:

> *There was no kind of safety in the mine. . . . After you take the coal out, you have to pull the posts out. You have to know whether it's "boom, boom" you hear—that's a fall going to come. Them posts starts cracking, you go. Oh yes, you get a warning. But I see them take out lots of good guys—young fellows died. If you kill a mule, you got fired. But if you kill a man, nothing. Because they had to buy a mule. They don't have to buy a man.*[4]

The hard work of the immigrants was often rewarded. Many of them saved every penny they possibly could. With these savings—and sometimes also with loans from other

Many children
worked in coal mines.
Young boys worked
for ten or twelve
hours a day picking
out pieces of slate that
had become mixed
in with the coal.

Other children
worked in factories.
This young boy
worked long hours
in a glass factory.

immigrants in their ethnic group—they eventually opened small stores or started businesses. It was common for families to work together in a store. For people who had fled poverty in the old country, being able to own even a small business was a thrilling experience.

Immigrants tended to move to places where their countrymen lived. Many immigrant groups lived in large cities, where they squeezed into apartment buildings called *tenements*, which were built without any thought to the renters' comfort or health. The toilet was in the hallway and was shared by all the families who lived on the floor. The rooms were often small, dark, and sunless. The tub was in the kitchen.

If something broke, the landlord did not always repair it. To make matters much worse, to make ends meet tenants often took in boarders, who slept in the kitchen or in any corner they could find. In the summertime, people slept on rooftops and fire escapes to get away from the stifling heat of these apartments.

To make extra money, families often worked at home. Kitchens and bedrooms might be filled with sewing machines on which men, women, and children would work until late at night. Sometimes, a whole floor of a tenement would be rented out and its tiny rooms converted into workshops. Because of their terrible conditions, these workplaces became known as "sweatshops."

Life was difficult for many of the immigrants, but it was not without its joys. Each immigrant group created its own community in America. In their neighborhoods they could eat the foods they were accustomed to, find newspapers written in their own language, listen to music they liked, and, most important, meet and talk to people who knew their language and culture.

Although the immigrants were crowded into small

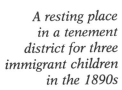

Life in tenement housing
was very often both
crowded and bleak
for the immigrants.

A resting place
in a tenement
district for three
immigrant children
in the 1890s

Daily immigrant life around the turn of the century

Immigrants on Mulberry Street in New York City around 1900

Immigrant iron workers at the Erie City Iron Works assembled for Americanization class after working hours.

Although life was hard for the immigrants, here on Coney Island in the 1890s they entertain themselves with music and dancing.

apartments, the streets were also their home. Adults socialized outside; children played stickball, jumping rope, and other games until sundown. With no television or radio, people found other ways to entertain themselves. The libraries were full of young and old alike. On the Lower East Side in Manhattan, where a large percentage of Jewish immigrants lived, lectures on science, literature, politics, and every other possible subject were popular. After working all day, many immigrants went to school at night to learn English.

As the immigrants ceaselessly worked to improve their lives, there were a growing number of Americans who hated the idea that "foreigners" were landing on "their" shores. Gradually, their voices became so strong that the doors to America started to close. It would take these voices of hate and fear over twenty years, but eventually they would succeed in closing those doors completely.

Chapter Four
THE DOORS CLOSE

For most turn-of-the-century immigrants who arrived in America, the first sight of their new home was the Statue of Liberty off the tip of Manhattan. At the base of this 152-foot-high (46 m) statue of a woman whose raised arm holds a lighted torch and at whose feet is a broken chain are these words:

> Give me your tired, your poor,
> Your huddled masses yearning to breathe free,
> The wretched refuse of your teeming shore,
> Send these, the homeless, tempest-tossed, to me:
> I lift my lamp beside the golden door.

This poem was written in 1883 for the immigrants who were then flooding the country. This was, it said, a country that welcomed all those who sought a better life for themselves. The author, Emma Lazarus, was herself a child of immigrants.

The Statue of Liberty, a welcoming sight for immigrants

Once here, immigrants sent home photographs and letters that encouraged entire families and groups from their home villages to emigrate to America.

The immigrants would not disappoint the nation. They and their children and grandchildren made great contributions to American society. They became doctors who found cures for disease, scientists who made important inventions. They opened stores, built streets and railroads, sewed clothing, and made shoes. They sent their children to war to fight for the United States; many were wounded or never returned at all.

But even as new immigrants continued to arrive, Emma Lazarus's words no longer spoke the truth. A growing number of Americans (whose own ancestors had not been born here!) resented the newcomers. They could not look past the immigrants' poverty. They never noticed that in their small, run-down apartments and homes these people were full of energy, dreams, and plans—and that these plans would help bring even more prosperity and success to the nation. Instead, they only saw the different customs and clothes and only heard the many different languages that they could not understand. How could these immigrants possibly be good enough to be Americans?

There was also a fear of different religions. Up until this time, the United States had been a largely Protestant country. Now, more Catholics and Jews were becoming Americans, too. Finally, many Americans feared that immigrants would take jobs away from them—especially during bad times, when jobs were scarce for everyone.

The press reflected many people's negative attitudes toward the newcomers. "The average immigrants are of course not only far below the average American in intellect, but are physically inferior," stated an article in the magazine *Popular Science Monthly*. The author went on to make suggestions as to how the immigrant children who attended American schools "can be assimilated without detriment to the natives."[1]

Newspapers and magazines printed articles with insulting stereotypes. In 1880, when a boat called the *Italia* arrived from Italy with a smallpox epidemic among the immigrants, a reporter for *The New York Times* wrote:

> *. . . there can be no doubt that the interests of the City, State, and nation demand that on the arrival of a steam-ship with a steerage full of immigrants like those brought by the* Italia, *the filthy, wretched, lazy, ignorant, and criminal dregs of the meanest sections of Italy, and infected with a terrible disease into the bargain, the authorities of the port should have power to compel her master to take back his cargo whence he got it with the least possible delay.*[2]

Another newspaper, *The New York Tribune*, wrote in the late 1800s that Jews "were accustomed to taking only one bath a year."

The prejudice against the immigrants took many forms. Some Americans tried to keep the newcomers out of their clubs, schools, restaurants, and neighborhoods. On October 11, 1906, for example, the San Francisco Board of Education issued an order which excluded all Chinese, Japanese, and Korean children from neighborhood schools and sent them to special schools just for Asians.

Some businesses were afraid that immigrants would open stores and restaurants that would take away their customers. Greek and Chinese immigrants, for example, worked hard to save money and open up restaurants, which were very popular—but not, of course, with other restaurant owners. A headline in an Arizona labor journal in the early 1900s read: "Greek Peril Confronts Phoenix Merchants." The article began: "Here we have in Phoenix three individuals, brothers, who have grown from one small little business house until they now own or control FIVE big establishments. These with the Chinese restaurants constitute a menace to the economic possibilities of Phoenix. They are a menace to YOU." At about the same time, a Santa Rosa, California, newspaper carried the following ad: "John's Restaurant, Pure American. No Rats, No Greeks."

The major newspaper in San Francisco, the *Chronicle*, ran headlines such as "Japanese a Menace to American Women," "Brown Men an Evil in the Public Schools," and "Brown Artisans Steal Brains of Whites."

To make sure that an immigrant or anyone else who was different from themselves didn't move next door, special restrictions were put into apartment and house leases and deeds.

In Fresno, California, where about 100,000 Armenians had settled, leases often had clauses that prohibited the property from being "occupied by any Negro, Chinese, Japanese, Hindu, Armenian, Asiatic, or native of the Turkish Empire or descendant of the above named persons, or anyone not of the white or Caucasian race." Fresno real estate brokers openly advertised property with such restrictions. (These restrictive land covenants, as they were called, were in use throughout the country until the United States Supreme Court declared them unconstitutional in 1948.) Armenians were also discriminated against or kept out of the city's churches and civic organizations.

Jewish immigrants also faced discrimination. They were barred from many summer resorts (it was not uncommon for a hotel to put up a sign saying "No Jews Allowed"), and were kept out of clubs and fraternities. The Jewish immigrants, who had an unusual thirst for learning and education, were especially affected by quotas that set a limit on the number of Jewish students allowed to attend many colleges and universities.

Beginning in the late 1800s, organizations began to form that tried to turn the country against the immigrants.

Resentment and fear of the foreign newcomers resulted in negative articles and cartoons in magazines and newspapers.

Some Americans even tried to keep the immigrants out of their neighborhoods.

Some immigrants, like the Japanese children in San Francisco, were excluded from the public schools. This photograph pictures the first move in a court suit that tested the constitutionality of this exclusion. A nine-year-old Japanese schoolboy is being refused admission to a public school.

In 1894 a group of New Englanders founded the Immigration Restriction League. The League was made up of men and women whose ancestors had come from England. They believed that they were better than the newest immigrants, and they tried to convince other Americans—and Congress—to stop the flow of people from eastern and southern Europe. Hate organizations such as the Ku Klux Klan raged against Catholics and Jews, accusing them of ridiculous plots such as trying to take over the government. Labor organizations blamed the country's problems on immigrants, accusing them of responsibility for lower wages and increased unemployment among native-born Americans.

Groups that opposed immigration influenced Congress, where a debate was taking place over whom to allow into the country and whom to exclude.

In 1882, Congress passed two immigration laws. The first, the Chinese Exclusion Act, was meant to stop Chinese workers from coming into the country for ten years. It barred all Chinese from entering the United States unless they were businessmen, government officials, students, teachers, or tourists. The other immigration law excluded "lunatics, idiots, convicts, and those likely to become public charges."

Congress passed more and more bills limiting who could enter the country. In 1907 a law was passed barring imbeciles, the feebleminded, persons with physical or mental abilities that could affect their ability to earn a living, and anyone under the age of sixteen who was unaccompanied by parents. An agreement was even signed between the United States and Japan in which it was agreed that no more passports would be issued to Japanese citizens.

There were some Congressmen, of course, who recognized the accomplishments of the new Americans. Representative Samuel McMillan of New York said in a speech to Congress in 1908:

> *I ask where would your furnaces have been puddled, where would your mines have been dug and worked, where would your great iron industries and constructions . . . have been were it not for the immigrants? . . . It is the immigrant that bears the burden of hard labor, toiling in the under stratums of labor rejected by the American workmen, and fills his mission and has contributed his full share to the building of our great country.*

But his words and those of others were not heard by the majority of the nation's lawmakers.

In 1917, Congress tried to stop the wave of immigrants by passing a bill (overriding a veto by President Woodrow Wilson) that required all immigrants to be able to read a forty-word passage in any language. To the disappointment of anti-immigrationists, this law did not stop the flow of newcomers. Many eager immigrants were able to learn to read and write at home and were able to pass the test.

America's entry into World War I helped the anti-immigration forces. With thousands of American boys being wounded and dying in Europe, it was easier to rally people against the European-born immigrants, although by now many were loyal American citizens. It was even argued that some immigrants might become spies for their former homelands.

After the war, the country was afraid of many of the political ideas—communism, anarchism, and socialism—that were brewing in Europe. Thousands of people were accused of being political radicals and were considered dangerous to the country. Without a fair trial, thousands of innocent people, many of them immigrants, were put in jail; 1,000 were sent to Ellis Island and deported.

Finally, Congress passed the Emergency Quota Act in

Despite the prejudice against the newcomers, immigrants on New York's Orchard Street help the war effort by buying war savings stamps and certificates in 1918.

In New York City, soon after the outbreak of World War I, many immigrants take the oath of allegiance to the United States.

Other immigrants enriched their communities by running successful businesses such as the butcher shop and clothing factory pictured here.

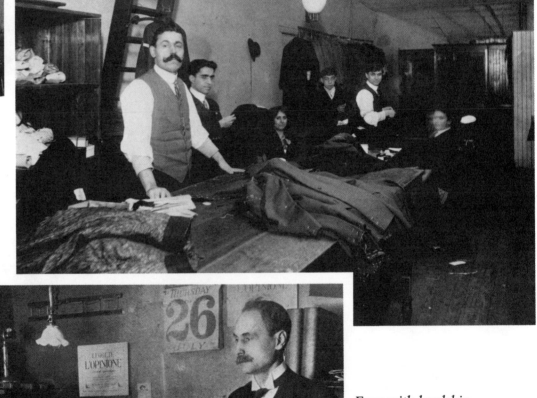

Even with hardship and exclusion, immigrants became successful members of their communities. An Italian newspaper run by and for Italians is pictured here.

Some of the many famous Ellis Island immigrants: film star Claudette Colbert from France; Supreme Court Justice Felix Frankfurter from Austria; political figure Emma Goldman from Russia; inventor of the helicopter, Igor Sikorsky, from the Ukraine

Immigrants with the same dreams as those who preceded them taking the oath of allegiance today

1921. Only 350,000 immigrants a year could now come into the United States—and there was a quota of immigrants from each country. Instead of 783,000, now only 155,000 people from southern and eastern Europe, for example, could enter the United States.

In 1924, Congress went even further. It set the maximum number of immigrants who could come into the country at about 150,000. The number of immigrants of any nationality who could be admitted was limited to 2 percent of the number of that nationality who lived in the United States in 1890. That meant that only 5,802 Italians, 2,784 Russians, and 307 Greeks would be allowed in. The law also denied permanent admission to the United States to all people from Africa and Asia.

The great wave of immigration was over. Forty-one years later, in 1965, a new law was passed by Congress, and immigrants from around the world once again began to arrive in America. Since then Congress has enacted other legislation that is designed to allow more and more immigrants into the country. Nevertheless, there are still long lists of people from many countries who are waiting for permission to come here.

Today, the immigrants arrive by plane instead of boat and carry suitcases instead of bundles on their backs. And instead of Europeans, Hispanics and Asians make up the largest number of newcomers. But their dreams—to work hard and build a better life for themselves—are no different from those of the immigrants who landed on Ellis Island nearly 100 years ago. In the process, these new immigrants, too, will build a better America.

Source Notes

Chapter One
1. Ellis Island Immigration Museum, Ellis Island, New York City.
2. Irving Howe, *World of Our Fathers* (New York: Harcourt Brace Jovanovich, 1976), p. 27.
3. Howe, p. 34.
4. Michael La Sorte, *La Merica: Images of Italian Greenhorn Experience* (Philadelphia: Temple University Press, 1985), p. 7.

Chapter Two
1. Ellis Island Immigration Museum, Ellis Island, New York City.

Chapter Three
1. Joan Morris and Charlotte Fox Zablusky, *American Mosaic: The Immigrant Experience in the Words of Those Who Lived It* (New York: E. P. Dutton, 1980), p. 10.
2. Isaac Metzkerf, ed., *Bintel Brief* (New York, Berhman, 1982), p. 11.
3. Alexander Alland, Sr., *Jacob A. Riis: Photographer & Citizen* (New York, Aperture, 1972), p. 172.
4. Morris and Zablusky, p. 56.

Chapter Four
1. *Popular Science Monthly*, January 1903, pp. 234–35.
2. *New York Times*, December 18, 1880, p. 4.

Index